הִנְּנִי

THE NEW HEBREW THROUGH PRAYER

WORKBOOK
3

Roberta Osser Baum

Cover and Book Design: Itzhack Shelomi
Project Editor: Terry S. Kaye

Springfield, New Jersey
www.behrmanhouse.com
ISBN 0-87441-138-6
ufactured in the United States of America

LESSON 1

אֵין כָּמוֹךָ \ אַב הָרַחֲמִים

Introducing the Torah Service

אֵין כָּמוֹךָ and אַב הָרַחֲמִים, the opening prayers in the Torah service, praise God. Traditionally, we acknowledge God as the source of the Torah. We declare that God is unique and we put our trust in God.

Complete the English phrases using the words below.

deeds like Yours   and Your reign   like You   Your sovereignty

1. אֵין <u>כָּמוֹךָ</u> בָאֱלֹהִים, יְיָ

There is none _____________, Adonai, among the gods (other people worship)

2. וְאֵין <u>כְּמַעֲשֶׂיךָ</u>.

and there are no _____________________

3. <u>מַלְכוּתְךָ</u> מַלְכוּת כָּל עוֹלָמִים

_____________________ is an eternal sovereignty

4. <u>וּמֶמְשַׁלְתְּךָ</u> בְּכָל דּוֹר וָדֹר.

_____________________ is from generation to generation.

Word Endings

What is the common suffix or word ending in the underlined Hebrew words above? _____

What does this suffix mean? _____________________________

FINAL LETTERS

Five letters have final forms: מ ם נ ן צ ץ פ ף כ ך

Add the final form to each word below.

Then read each complete line aloud.

1. עוֹלָמִי___ יְרוּשָׁלַיִ___ הָרַחֲמִי___ חַיִּי___ אַלְפַּיִ___ ם

2. אָמֵ___ וְאֵי___ יִתֵּ___ הָרַחֲמָ___ צִיּוֹ___ ן

3. עֵ___ הָאָרֶ___ אֶרֶ___ חָפֵ___ חָמֵ___ ץ

4. יוֹסֵ___ אָלֶ___ לְהִתְעַטֵּ___ מוּסָ___ יַחֲלִי___ ף

5. מֶלֶ___ יְבָרֵ___ יִמְלֹ___ בְּרִי___ אֱלֹהַיִ___ ךְ

6. בִּרְצוֹנְ___ כָּמוֹ___ מַעֲשֶׂי___ עַבְדְּ___ שְׁלֹמֶ___ ךּ

WORD POWER

Write the Hebrew words from the lines above next to the matching English meaning.

Joseph ________________	Jerusalem ________________
life ________________	*alef* ________________
Amen ________________	ruler ________________

RECOGNIZING ROOTS

Connect each root to its matching English word.

mercy	עשה
make	מלכ
rule	רחמ

Read the words in each line below.

Write the root for each word: עשה מלכ רחמ

1. לְמַעֲשֵׂה מַלְכוּת כְּמַעֲשֶׂיךָ רַחֲמִים

__ __ __ __ __ __ __ __ __ __ __ __

2. וְרַחוּם יִמְלֹךְ יַעֲשֶׂה מַלְכֵּנוּ

__ __ __ __ __ __ __ __ __ __ __ __

GOD'S NAME

Below are four phrases that refer to God. In each Hebrew phrase circle the word built on the root רחמ.

Merciful Parent	אַב הָרַחֲמִים
God full of mercy	אֵל מָלֵא רַחֲמִים
the merciful One	הָרַחֲמָן
compassionate and gracious God	אֵל חַנּוּן וְרַחוּם

Write the phrase that is also the name of a prayer in the Torah service.

____

READING RULE

The דָּגֵשׁ

The דָּגֵשׁ is a dot sometimes found in the middle of a Hebrew letter.
The דָּגֵשׁ changes the sound of these family letters:

ב בּ   כ כּ   פ פּ

Many times the דָּגֵשׁ does *not* change the sound of a letter. Practice reading the letters below.

גּ דּ הּ וּ זּ טּ יּ לּ

מּ נּ סּ צּ ק שּׁ שּׂ

Which letter looks like the vowel "oo"? ________

Read the letters below and circle those with sounds that change when a דָּגֵשׁ is added, for example, בּ.

1. דּ מּ גּ בּ ק סּ פּ
2. לּ נּ תּ צּ כּ יּ בּ
3. שּׁ זּ ט פּ הּ וּ כּ

SIDDUR PHRASES

Circle each word with a דָּגֵשׁ in the following phrases. Read each complete phrase.

1. כִּי בְךָ לְבַד בָּטָחְנוּ
2. יְיָ יְבָרֵךְ אֶת עַמּוֹ בַשָּׁלוֹם
3. וְהַעֲמִידֵנוּ מַלְכֵּנוּ לְחַיִּים
4. בִּרְצוֹנְךָ אֶת צִיּוֹן
5. הָאֵל הַנֶּאֱמָן בְּכָל דְּבָרָיו
6. מֶלֶךְ אֵל רָם וְנִשָּׂא

VERSES FROM TORAH

The Five Books of Moses

Genesis | Exodus | Leviticus | Numbers | Deuteronomy

Read these verses from the story of creation.
Circle the Hebrew word for God—אֱלֹהִים—in each excerpt.

1. בְּרֵאשִׁית בָּרָא אֱלֹהִים אֵת הַשָּׁמַיִם וְאֵת הָאָרֶץ...וַיֹּאמֶר אֱלֹהִים
יְהִי אוֹר וַיְהִי אוֹר. (Genesis 1:1, 3)

In the beginning God created the heavens and the earth…God said, "Let there be light." And there was light.

2. וַיַּעַשׂ אֱלֹהִים אֶת הָרָקִיעַ...וַיִּקְרָא אֱלֹהִים לָרָקִיעַ
שָׁמָיִם... (Genesis 1:7, 8)

And God made the expanse…and God called the expanse sky…

3. וַיִּקְרָא אֱלֹהִים לַיַּבָּשָׁה אֶרֶץ...וַתּוֹצֵא הָאָרֶץ דֶּשֶׁא... (Genesis 1:10, 12)

And God called the dry land earth…the earth brought forth vegetation…

4. וַיַּעַשׂ אֱלֹהִים אֶת שְׁנֵי הַמְּאֹרֹת הַגְּדֹלִים...
וְאֵת הַכּוֹכָבִים. (Genesis 1:16)

And God made the two great sources of light…and the stars.

5. וַיֹּאמֶר אֱלֹהִים יִשְׁרְצוּ הַמַּיִם שֶׁרֶץ נֶפֶשׁ חַיָּה וְעוֹף יְעוֹפֵף
עַל הָאָרֶץ... (Genesis 1:20)

And God said, "Let the waters bring forth swarms of living creatures, and birds that fly over the earth…"

6. וַיֹּאמֶר אֱלֹהִים תּוֹצֵא הָאָרֶץ נֶפֶשׁ חַיָּה...וַיִּבְרָא אֱלֹהִים אֶת הָאָדָם בְּצַלְמוֹ...זָכָר וּנְקֵבָה בָּרָא אֹתָם. (Genesis 1:24, 27)

And God said, "Let the earth bring forth every kind of living creature..." And God created male and female humans in the image of God.

7. ...וַיִּשְׁבֹּת בַּיּוֹם הַשְּׁבִיעִי מִכָּל מְלַאכְתּוֹ אֲשֶׁר עָשָׂה. וַיְבָרֶךְ אֱלֹהִים אֶת יוֹם הַשְּׁבִיעִי וַיְקַדֵּשׁ אֹתוֹ... (Genesis 2:2–3)

...And God rested on the seventh day from all the work God had made. And God blessed the seventh day, and made it holy...

Think About It!

In what way does the prayer below refer to the story of creation?

אֵין כָּמוֹךָ בָאֱלֹהִים, יְיָ, וְאֵין כְּמַעֲשֶׂיךָ.

There is none like You, Adonai, among the gods (other people worship), and there are no deeds like Yours.

___

___

___

READING RULE

The Sh'va

At the beginning of a word or word-part, the *sh'va* (ְ) is always sounded.
Its sound is "a" as in "alone."

לְ עַמּוֹ   מְ בֹרָךְ   פְּ תִיל

In the middle of a word and at the end of a syllable, the *sh'va* is often silent.
The letter over the *sh'va* is blended with the letter-vowel combination that comes before it.

מִקְ דָּשׁ   יִשְׂ רָאֵל

When a *sh'va* appears in the middle of a word under two adjacent letters (ְ ְ), the first *sh'va* is silent and follows the reading rule of the silent *sh'va*.
The second *sh'va* is sounded and follows the reading rule of the sounded *sh'va*.

נַפְ שְׁךָ   יִשְׂ מְחוּ   תִּזְ כְּרוּ

WORD BUILDING

Read each word-part aloud.
Put the word-parts together and read the whole word.

1. יִמְ לֹךְ   יִמְלֹךְ
2. בָּ טָחְ נוּ   בָּטָחְנוּ
3. בִּרְ צוֹנְ ךָ   בִּרְצוֹנְךָ
4. בְּ אַרְ צֵ נוּ   בְּאַרְצֵנוּ
5. חַסְ דְּ ךָ   חַסְדְּךָ
6. כְּ מִשְׁ פְּ חוֹת   כְּמִשְׁפְּחוֹת
7. בְּ שִׁבְ תְּ ךָ   בְּשִׁבְתְּךָ
8. וּ מֶמְ שַׁלְ תְּ ךָ   וּמֶמְשַׁלְתְּךָ

יִשְׂמְחוּ

The Shabbat morning עֲמִידָה consists of seven blessings. The fourth, or middle, blessing of the Shabbat morning עֲמִידָה is called קְדוּשַּׁת הַיּוֹם, the Holiness of the Day.

Which day in the week is holy? Write your answer in Hebrew. ____________

Practice reading יִשְׂמְחוּ, a part of קְדוּשַּׁת הַיּוֹם in some services.

1. יִשְׂמְחוּ בְמַלְכוּתְךָ שׁוֹמְרֵי שַׁבָּת וְקוֹרְאֵי עֹנֶג. עַם מְקַדְּשֵׁי שְׁבִיעִי

2. כֻּלָּם יִשְׂבְּעוּ וְיִתְעַנְּגוּ מִטּוּבֶךָ. וְהַשְּׁבִיעִי רָצִיתָ בּוֹ וְקִדַּשְׁתּוֹ.

3. חֶמְדַּת יָמִים אוֹתוֹ קָרָאתָ, זֵכֶר לְמַעֲשֵׂה בְרֵאשִׁית.

Word Study

Complete the following activities using the יִשְׂמְחוּ above.

- Circle the two words that have a double *sh'va.*
- Underline any three words with a *dagesh* that does not change the sound of the letter.
- Write the words built on the following roots:

מלכ ______________ עשה ______________

כִּי מִצִּיּוֹן \ לְךָ יְיָ

Taking the Torah from the Ark

The Torah service is the highlight of the Shabbat morning service. It consists of three parts: taking the Torah from the Ark, reading from the Torah, and returning the Torah to the Ark. We stand as the Torah service begins and as the Torah is carried among the people of the congregation.

Below is the prayer we sing as the Torah is removed from the Ark. Write the missing Hebrew words above the English meanings.

שֶׁנָּתַן מִירוּשָׁלָיִם תּוֹרָה

בִּקְדֻשָּׁתוֹ מִצִּיּוֹן לְעַמּוֹ וּדְבַר

1. כִּי __________ תֵּצֵא __________, __________ יְיָ __________.

(for out of Zion / Torah / and the word of / from Jerusalem)

2. בָּרוּךְ __________ תּוֹרָה __________ יִשְׂרָאֵל __________.

(who gave / to God's people / in God's holiness)

Did You Know?

The root שלם means more than "peace." It means "harmony," "completeness," or "wholeness."

Circle the root שלם in the word יְרוּשָׁלַיִם ("city of peace").

PREFIX וְ

The prefix וְ means "and." It is attached to the beginning of a word. The prefix may also look like this: וּ   וַ   וָ   וִ

WORD BUILDING

We sing לְךָ יְיָ when we take the Torah from the Ark and carry it among the congregants. The following words from לְךָ יְיָ have the prefix meaning "and." Read the words.

1. וְהַהוֹד
2. וּבָאָרֶץ
3. וְהַנֵּצַח
4. וְהַגְּבוּרָה
5. וְהַתִּפְאֶרֶת
6. וְהַמִּתְנַשֵּׂא

READING RULE

Vav with a Dagesh

When the letter ו has a *dagesh* (וּ), it looks like the vowel "oo" (וּ) or the prefix "oo" (וּ). Two clues tell us when וּ is the letter *vav* with a *dagesh*:

1. If the letter *preceding* וּ already has a vowel (צִוָּה), it's a *vav*.
   Write the letter *preceding* וּ with its vowel in the word צִוָּה. ___
2. If וּ has its own vowel (צִוָּה), it's a *vav*.
   Write the letter וּ with its vowel in the word צִוָּה. ___

Add a *dagesh* to the letter *vav* in each word below.
Then read the words.

מְצַוְךָ   קִוִינוּ   כַּוָנָה   צִוָה   מְקַוִים

RECOGNIZING THE ROOT קדשׁ

Many words in the סִדּוּר are built on the root קדשׁ ("holy").

Write the root. ___ ___ ___

Rhythm Reading

Read aloud the words built on the root קדשׁ in the lines below.

1. קָדוֹשׁ   קֹדֶשׁ   קָדְשׁוֹ   קָדְשְׁךָ

2. קִדּוּשׁ   קַדִּישׁ   קְדֻשָּׁה   קְדֹשִׁים

3. קְדוּשַּׁת   קִדַּשְׁתָּ   וּקְדוֹשִׁים   שֶׁמַּקְדִּישִׁים

HOLY PLACES, HOLY OBJECTS, HOLY TIME

Write the letters קדשׁ in the blank spaces in each word below. Then read the complete word.

1. אֲרוֹן ___ ___ֹ___ֶ ___ Holy Ark

2. אֶרֶץ הַ___ֹ___ֶ ___ holy land

3. עִיר הַ___ֹ___ֶ ___ holy city

4. לְשׁוֹן הַ___ֹ___ֶ ___ holy language

5. בֵּית הַמִּ___ְ___ָ ___ Holy Temple

6. ___ִ___וּ___ Kiddush

Think About It!

What is the name of the holy land? ______________________________

the holy city? ______________________________

the holy language? ______________________________

SELECTIONS FROM THE קִדּוּשׁ

קִדּוּשׁ means "make holy" or "sanctify."
Reciting the קִדּוּשׁ helps to make Shabbat holy.
The phrases below are selections from the קִדּוּשׁ.
Circle the word in each phrase built on the root קדשׁ.
Read each circled word aloud. Then read each phrase aloud.

1. אֲשֶׁר קִדְּשָׁנוּ בְּמִצְוֹתָיו וְרָצָה בָנוּ
2. וְשַׁבַּת קָדְשׁוֹ בְּאַהֲבָה וּבְרָצוֹן הִנְחִילָנוּ
3. כִּי הוּא יוֹם תְּחִלָּה לְמִקְרָאֵי קֹדֶשׁ
4. כִּי בָנוּ בָחַרְתָּ וְאוֹתָנוּ קִדַּשְׁתָּ מִכָּל הָעַמִּים
5. וְשַׁבַּת קָדְשְׁךָ בְּאַהֲבָה וּבְרָצוֹן הִנְחַלְתָּנוּ
6. בָּרוּךְ אַתָּה יְיָ מְקַדֵּשׁ הַשַּׁבָּת

Blessing Bee

The קִדּוּשׁ begins with the blessing over wine.
Write the words below in the correct order to complete the blessing over wine.

פְּרִי בּוֹרֵא הַגָּפֶן

בָּרוּךְ אַתָּה יְיָ אֱלֹהֵינוּ מֶלֶךְ הָעוֹלָם ______ ______ ______.

VERSES FROM TORAH

The Five Books of Moses

Genesis | **Exodus** | **Leviticus** | **Numbers** | **Deuteronomy**

Read these verses from the story of the burning bush.

1. ...וַיַּרְא וְהִנֵּה הַסְּנֶה בֹּעֵר בָּאֵשׁ וְהַסְּנֶה אֵינֶנּוּ אֻכָּל. (Exodus 3:2)

...And he (Moses) looked, and behold the bush burned with fire, yet the bush was not consumed.

2. ...וַיִּקְרָא אֵלָיו אֱלֹהִים מִתּוֹךְ הַסְּנֶה וַיֹּאמֶר מֹשֶׁה מֹשֶׁה
וַיֹּאמֶר הִנֵּנִי. (Exodus 3:4)

...And God called to him (Moses) out of the midst of the bush saying, "Moses, Moses." And he (Moses) said, "Here I am."

3. וַיֹּאמֶר...הַמָּקוֹם אֲשֶׁר אַתָּה עוֹמֵד עָלָיו אַדְמַת־קֹדֶשׁ
הוּא. (Exodus 3:5)

And (God) said..."The place on which you are standing is holy ground."

4. וַיֹּאמֶר יְהוָֹה רָאֹה רָאִיתִי אֶת עֳנִי עַמִּי אֲשֶׁר בְּמִצְרָיִם... (Exodus 3:7)

And Adonai said, "I have seen the afflictions of My people in Egypt..."

5. ...וְהוֹצֵא אֶת עַמִּי בְנֵי יִשְׂרָאֵל מִמִּצְרָיִם. (Exodus 3:10)

"...And you will free My people, the children of Israel, from Egypt."

Here I Am: הִנֵּנִי

When God first called upon Abraham and, generations later, when God called upon Moses, both responded with הִנֵּנִי, "Here I am." Their answer indicated their readiness to serve God.

Why do you think this Hebrew series is called הִנֵּנִי?

מִזְמוֹר לְדָוִד

The congregation chants Psalm 29, מִזְמוֹר לְדָוִד, during the procession to return the Torah to the Ark. The psalm praises the "voice of God," קוֹל יְיָ, for its power and majesty. Read these selections from Psalm 29.

1. קוֹל יְיָ עַל הַמָּיִם — *The voice of Adonai is above the waters.*
2. קוֹל יְיָ בַּכֹּחַ — *The voice of Adonai is mighty.*
3. קוֹל יְיָ בֶּהָדָר — *The voice of Adonai is full of majesty.*
4. קוֹל יְיָ שֹׁבֵר אֲרָזִים — *The voice of Adonai breaks cedars.*
5. קוֹל יְיָ חֹצֵב לַהֲבוֹת אֵשׁ — *The voice of Adonai sparks fiery flames.*
6. קוֹל יְיָ יָחִיל מִדְבָּר — *The voice of Adonai makes the desert tremble.*
7. קוֹל יְיָ יְחוֹלֵל אַיָּלוֹת — *The voice of Adonai makes the rams dance.*
8. יְיָ עֹז לְעַמּוֹ יִתֵּן, יְיָ יְבָרֵךְ אֶת עַמּוֹ בַשָּׁלוֹם.

Adonai will give strength to God's people, Adonai will bless God's people with peace.

God's Voice

How does one *hear* "the voice of Adonai"?

____

____

בְּרְכוֹת הַתּוֹרָה

Torah Blessings

On Shabbat, the Torah portion is divided into seven readings known as עֲלִיּוֹת. A blessing is recited before and after each reading. The blessing before the Torah reading praises God for choosing the Jewish people to receive the Torah. The blessing after the reading praises God for the truth of Torah and eternal life.

The blessing before the Torah reading begins with the בָּרְכוּ.

בָּרְכוּ אֶת־יְיָ הַמְבֹרָךְ.
בָּרוּךְ יְיָ הַמְבֹרָךְ לְעוֹלָם וָעֶד.

It continues with the following words:

בָּרוּךְ אַתָּה יְיָ אֱלֹהֵינוּ מֶלֶךְ הָעוֹלָם...

The English phrases below are in the correct order. Complete the blessing by numbering the Hebrew phrases to match the English. The first one has been done for you.

1. for choosing us	וְנָתַן־לָנוּ	___
2. from all the nations	נוֹתֵן הַתּוֹרָה	___
3. and giving us	אֲשֶׁר בָּחַר בָּנוּ	1
4. God's Torah	בָּרוּךְ אַתָּה יְיָ	___
5. praised are You, Adonai	אֶת־תּוֹרָתוֹ	___
6. who gives us the Torah	מִכָּל־הָעַמִּים	___

The blessing after the Torah reading begins with the following words:

בָּרוּךְ אַתָּה יְיָ אֱלֹהֵינוּ מֶלֶךְ הָעוֹלָם...

The English phrases below are in the correct order. Complete the blessing by numbering the Hebrew phrases to match the English. The first one has been done for you.

1. who gave us	וְחַיֵּי עוֹלָם	___
2. the Torah of truth	נוֹתֵן הַתּוֹרָה	___
3. and implanted within us	אֲשֶׁר נָתַן לָנוּ	1
4. eternal life	נָטַע בְּתוֹכֵנוּ	___
5. praised are You, Adonai	תּוֹרַת אֱמֶת	___
6. who gives us the Torah	בָּרוּךְ אַתָּה יְיָ	___

Write the three forms of the word תּוֹרָה found in the blessings before and after the Torah reading. ____________ ____________ ____________

CONCLUDING SENTENCES

These sentences conclude the seven בְּרָכוֹת of the Shabbat morning עֲמִידָה.
Read each sentence fluently.

1. בָּרוּךְ אַתָּה יְיָ מָגֵן אַבְרָהָם\מָגֵן אַבְרָהָם וְעֶזְרַת שָׂרָה.
2. בָּרוּךְ אַתָּה יְיָ מְחַיֵּה הַכֹּל\הַמֵּתִים.
3. בָּרוּךְ אַתָּה יְיָ הָאֵל הַקָּדוֹשׁ.
4. בָּרוּךְ אַתָּה יְיָ מְקַדֵּשׁ הַשַּׁבָּת.
5. בָּרוּךְ אַתָּה יְיָ הַמַּחֲזִיר שְׁכִינָתוֹ לְצִיּוֹן.
6. בָּרוּךְ אַתָּה יְיָ הַטּוֹב שִׁמְךָ וּלְךָ נָאֶה לְהוֹדוֹת.
7. בָּרוּךְ אַתָּה יְיָ הַמְבָרֵךְ אֶת־עַמּוֹ יִשְׂרָאֵל בַּשָּׁלוֹם.

Write the number of the sentence which praises:

- God for the holiness of Shabbat #___
- God for the blessing of peace # ___

Remember This!

צִיּוֹן means "Zion." צִיּוֹן is the name of one of the hills in יְרוּשָׁלַיִם.
The term צִיּוֹן is also used as a name for the city of Jerusalem or the entire land of Israel.

RHYTHM READING

Read each set of words below. Then complete the activities that follow.

1. תּוֹרָתוֹ   תּוֹרָתֵנוּ   תּוֹרָתֶךָ
2. עַם   עַמּוֹ   הָעַמִּים
3. שָׁלוֹם   שְׁלֹמֹה   יְרוּשָׁלַיִם
4. אָמֵן   נֶאֱמָן   מַאֲמִין
5. עוֹלָם   לְעוֹלָם   עוֹלָמִים
6. חַי   חַיִּים   וְחַיֵּי
7. יִתְבָּרַךְ   הַמְבֹרָךְ   וּמְבָרְכִים
8. תִּקְוָה   הַתִּקְוָה   תִּקְוָתֵנוּ
9. צַדִּיק   צֶדֶק   צְדָקָה
10. נָתַן   נוֹתֵן   שֶׁנָּתַתָּ

Circle the name of the national anthem of the Jewish people.

Underline the word we say at the conclusion of a blessing.

Draw a box around the capital of Israel.

Put a ✡ star above a word built on the root ברכ.

Building a Blessing

Fill in the blanks by choosing words from Rhythm Reading above.

1. בָּרוּךְ יְיָ הַמְבֹרָךְ __________ וָעֶד
2. וְנָתַן־לָנוּ אֶת __________
3. אֲשֶׁר __________ לָנוּ תּוֹרַת אֱמֶת
4. __________ עוֹלָם נָטַע בְּתוֹכֵנוּ
5. בָּרוּךְ אַתָּה יְיָ, __________ תּוֹרָה

VERSES FROM TORAH

The Five Books of Moses

Genesis | Exodus | **Leviticus** | Numbers | Deuteronomy

The Torah portion קְדשִׁים is in the Book of Leviticus. What is the root of the word קְדשִׁים? ___ ___ ___ What is the English meaning? ____________

The mitzvot in קְדשִׁים show us how to behave in order to be a holy people.

Read the verses. Then answer the questions on the following page.

1. ...קְדשִׁים תִּהְיוּ כִּי קָדוֹשׁ אֲנִי יְהוָֹה אֱלֹהֵיכֶם. (Leviticus 19:2)

...You shall be holy for I, Adonai your God, am holy.

2. ...לֹא תְכַלֶּה פְּאַת שָׂדְךָ...וּפֶרֶט כַּרְמְךָ לֹא תְלַקֵּט לֶעָנִי וְלַגֵּר
תַּעֲזֹב אֹתָם אֲנִי יְהוָֹה אֱלֹהֵיכֶם. (Leviticus 19:9, 10)

...You shall not reap the corner of your field...you shall not gather the fallen fruit of your vineyard; you shall leave them for the poor and for the stranger. I am Adonai your God.

3. לֹא תֵלֵךְ רָכִיל בְּעַמֶּיךָ לֹא תַעֲמֹד עַל דַּם רֵעֶךָ
אֲנִי יְהוָֹה. (Leviticus 19:16)

You shall not be a talebearer among your people. You shall not stand idly by the blood of your neighbor. I am Adonai.

4. לֹא תִקֹּם וְלֹא תִטֹּר אֶת בְּנֵי עַמֶּךָ וְאָהַבְתָּ לְרֵעֲךָ כָּמוֹךָ
אֲנִי יְהוָֹה. (Leviticus 19:18)

You shall neither take vengeance nor bear a grudge against your own people, and you shall love your neighbor as yourself. I am Adonai.

5. וְכִי יָגוּר אִתְּךָ גֵּר בְּאַרְצְכֶם לֹא תוֹנוּ אֹתוֹ...כִּי־גֵרִים הֱיִיתֶם
בְּאֶרֶץ מִצְרָיִם אֲנִי יְהוָֹה אֱלֹהֵיכֶם. (Leviticus 19:33, 34)

And if a stranger lives with you in your land, you shall not do him wrong...for you were strangers in the land of Egypt. I, Adonai, am your God.

A HOLY PEOPLE

Complete the following activities using the verses from Leviticus on page 20.

Verse 1: Explain the meaning of "holy" in your own words.

____

Verse 2: Draw a rectangle—a "field"—in the space below. Mark off the corners. In each of the four corners, write one way you can help feed "the poor and the stranger" in today's times.

Verse 3: Draw a mouth in the space below. In it write one way gossip or telling tales can hurt others and one way it can hurt the "talebearer."

Verse 4: List three ways you can show respect for your "neighbor," your fellow human being.

(i) ____

(ii) ____

(iii) ____

Verse 5: Explain what happened to the Jewish people when they were strangers בְּאֶרֶץ מִצְרָיִם ("in the land of Egypt").

____

Why do you think we should remember that period in our history?

____

The Five Books of Moses

The Torah is also called the Five Books of Moses.
Read the Hebrew and English name of each book.

5. דְּבָרִים	4. בְּמִדְבַּר	3. וַיִּקְרָא	2. שְׁמוֹת	1. בְּרֵאשִׁית
Deuteronomy	Numbers	Leviticus	Exodus	Genesis

Write the names of the books in the Hebrew and English crossword puzzles below. Leave out the vowels in the Hebrew puzzle. Use the number of each book as your guide.

Hebrew Names

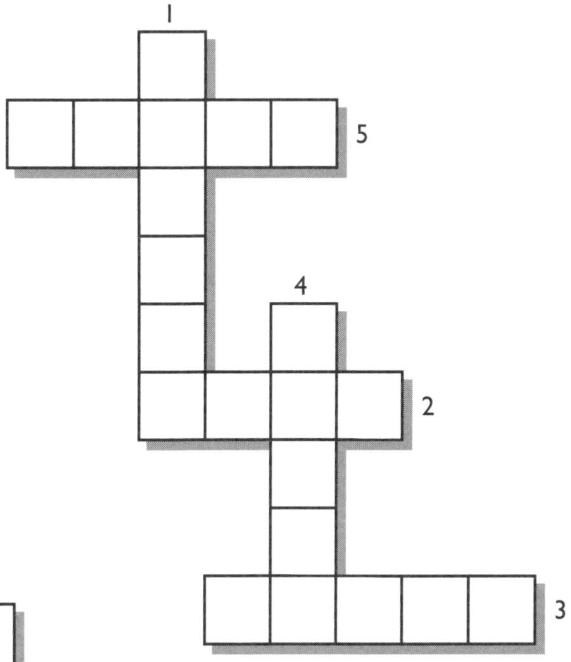

English Names

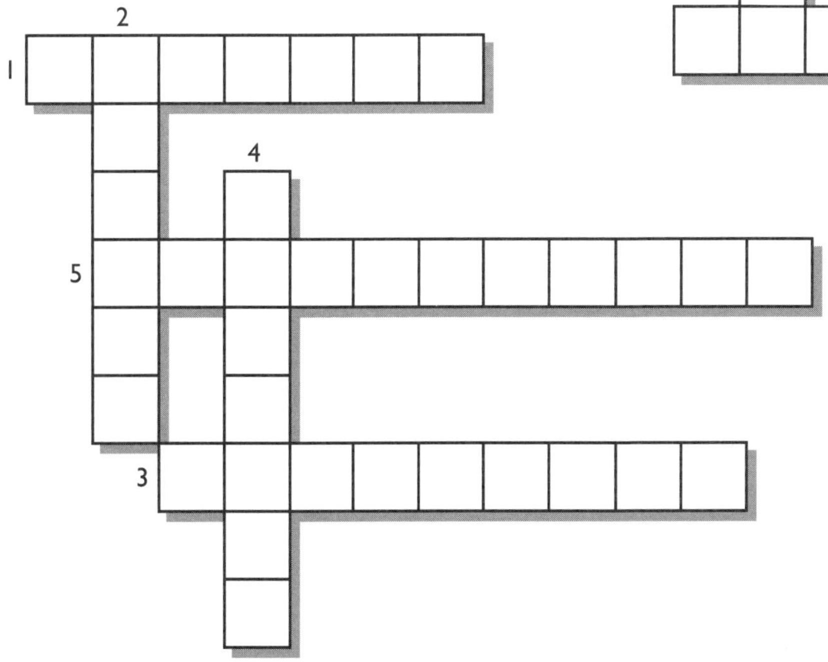

בִּרְכוֹת הַשַּׁחַר

The morning blessings, בִּרְכוֹת הַשַּׁחַר, are a part of the introductory morning prayers. This selection from the morning blessings thanks and acknowledges God for the good in the world.

Practice reading the blessings.

בָּרוּךְ אַתָּה, יְיָ אֱלֹהֵינוּ,	*Praised are You, Adonai our God,*
מֶלֶךְ הָעוֹלָם...	*Ruler of the world…*
1. שֶׁעָשַׂנִי יִשְׂרָאֵל	*who has made me a Jew*
2. פּוֹקֵחַ עִוְרִים	*who opens the eyes of the blind*
3. מַלְבִּישׁ עֲרֻמִּים	*who provides clothes for the naked*
4. מַתִּיר אֲסוּרִים	*who brings freedom to the captive*
5. זוֹקֵף כְּפוּפִים	*who lifts up the fallen*
6. הַמֵּכִין מִצְעֲדֵי גָבֶר	*who makes firm each person's steps*

Choose one of the blessings above and explain it in your own words. Write the number of the blessing you chose.

____

____

____

LESSON 4

בִּרְכוֹת הַהַפְטָרָה

Haftarah Blessings

The הַפְטָרָה reading is a selection from one of the books of נְבִיאִים (Prophets). Five haftarah blessings, בִּרְכוֹת הַהַפְטָרָה, accompany the reading—one before the reading and four after it. They reflect different aspects of Jewish belief.

Blessing Before the Haftarah Reading

The blessing before the haftarah praises God for the teaching of the prophets. Fill in the blanks in the blessing with the words from the list below. Then read the complete blessing.

בֶּאֱמֶת   וָצֶדֶק   עַבְדּוֹ   טוֹבִים   הַבּוֹחֵר

בִּנְבִיאִים   עַמּוֹ   הַנֶּאֱמָרִים   בָּחַר

1. בָּרוּךְ אַתָּה, יְיָ אֱלֹהֵינוּ, מֶלֶךְ הָעוֹלָם, אֲשֶׁר ______________
(chose)

2. ______________ (prophets) ______________ (good), וְרָצָה בְדִבְרֵיהֶם

______________ (spoken) ______________ (in truth).

3. בָּרוּךְ אַתָּה יְיָ, ______________ (the one who chooses) בַּתּוֹרָה, וּבְמֹשֶׁה ______________ (God's servant),

4. וּבְיִשְׂרָאֵל ______________ (God's people), וּבִנְבִיאֵי הָאֱמֶת ______________ (and righteousness).

MEET THE PROPHETS

Write the Hebrew name of each prophet next to the matching English name below.

הוֹשֵׁעַ יוֹאֵל עֹבַדְיָה יוֹנָה

חֲבַקּוּק דְּבוֹרָה חַגַּי מֹשֶׁה

Haggai	________	Deborah	________
Joel	________	Obadiah	________
Moses	________	Hosea	________
Jonah	________	Ḥabakkuk	________

MONTHS OF THE YEAR

Read the names of the twelve months of the Jewish year.

1. תִּשְׁרֵי
2. חֶשְׁוָן
3. כִּסְלֵו
4. טֵבֵת
5. שְׁבָט
6. אֲדָר
7. נִיסָן
8. אִיָּר
9. סִיוָן
10. תַּמּוּז
11. אָב
12. אֱלוּל

READING RULE

"Eye" Ending / "Ahv" Ending

The vowel sounds ָ and ַ followed by י at the end of a word have the sound "eye" (אֲדֹנָי, אֲבוֹתַי).

Add י to the following words to change the ending vowel sound to "eye." Then read each word.

שַׁדַ___ חַ___ שְׂפָתַ___ אֱלֹהַ___

When ו follows ָי or ַי at the end of a word, the combination ָיו or ַיו has the sound "ahv."

Add ו to change the ending vowel sound to "ahv." Then read each word.

יָדָי___ עֵינָי___ אֱלֹהַי___ רַגְלָי___ אֹהֲבָי___ בְּמִצְוֹתָי___

WORD BUILDING

Read each word-part. Then read each whole word.

1.	אִימָ	תַי	אִימָתַי
2.	רַבּוֹ	תַי	רַבּוֹתַי
3.	חֲבֵ	רַי	חֲבֵרַי
4.	דְּבָ	רָיו	דְּבָרָיו
5.	לִירֵ	אָיו	לִירֵאָיו
6.	בִּמְרוֹ	מָיו	בִּמְרוֹמָיו

Wise Words

Read this saying from the great teacher and sage Hillel (Pirke Avot 1:14).

If I am not for myself, who is for me? אִם אֵין אֲנִי לִי, מִי לִי?

And if I am only for myself, what am I? וּכְשֶׁאֲנִי לְעַצְמִי, מָה אֲנִי?

And if not now, when? וְאִם לֹא עַכְשָׁיו, אֵימָתַי?

What is Hillel teaching us? ______________________________

____

IN CONCLUSION

Below is the concluding sentence for each of the five haftarah blessings.

Read each one aloud and look for key words you know. Then write the number of the Hebrew sentence next to its matching English meaning.

1. בָּרוּךְ אַתָּה יְיָ, הַבּוֹחֵר בַּתּוֹרָה, וּבְמשֶׁה עַבְדּוֹ, וּבְיִשְׂרָאֵל עַמּוֹ, וּבִנְבִיאֵי הָאֱמֶת וָצֶדֶק.

2. בָּרוּךְ אַתָּה יְיָ, הָאֵל הַנֶּאֱמָן בְּכָל־דְּבָרָיו.

3. בָּרוּךְ אַתָּה יְיָ, מְשַׂמֵּחַ צִיּוֹן בְּבָנֶיהָ.

4. בָּרוּךְ אַתָּה יְיָ, מָגֵן דָּוִד.

5. בָּרוּךְ אַתָּה יְיָ, מְקַדֵּשׁ הַשַּׁבָּת.

___ Praised are You, Adonai, Shield of David.

___ Praised are You, Adonai, who makes Zion rejoice with her children.

___ Praised are You, Adonai, who sanctifies Shabbat.

___ Praised are You, Adonai, faithful in all your words.

___ Praised are You, Adonai, the One who takes delight in (chooses) the Torah, and in Moses, God's servant, and in Israel, God's people, and in the prophets of truth and righteousness (justice).

The Five Books of Moses

Genesis | Exodus | Leviticus | **Numbers** | Deuteronomy

Before the Israelites entered the land of Canaan, God told Moses to send twelve spies to scout out the land—one spy from each tribe. Read the following selection of verses from the Torah story about the twelve spies.

1. שְׁלַח לְךָ אֲנָשִׁים וְיָתֻרוּ אֶת אֶרֶץ כְּנַעַן אֲשֶׁר אֲנִי נֹתֵן לִבְנֵי יִשְׂרָאֵל... (Numbers 13:1–2)

Send men to scout the land of Canaan which I am giving to the children of Israel…

2. וּרְאִיתֶם אֶת הָאָרֶץ...וְאֶת הָעָם הַיֹּשֵׁב עָלֶיהָ הֶחָזָק הוּא הֲרָפֶה הַמְעַט הוּא אִם רָב. (Numbers 13:18)

And see the land…and whether the people who dwell in it are strong or weak, few or many.

3. וּמָה הָאָרֶץ אֲשֶׁר הוּא יֹשֵׁב בָּהּ הֲטוֹבָה הִיא אִם רָעָה... (Numbers 13:19)

And whether the land in which they dwell is good or bad….

4. וּמָה הָאָרֶץ הַשְּׁמֵנָה הִיא אִם רָזָה הֲיֵשׁ בָּהּ עֵץ אִם אַיִן... (Numbers 13:20)

And whether the land is rich or poor. Whether it is wooded or not…

Drawing Conclusions

Why were these facts about the land and its people important for Moses and the Israelites?

____

Why was one spy from each tribe sent to scout out the land?

____

בָּרוּךְ שֶׁאָמַר

בָּרוּךְ שֶׁאָמַר is a series of blessings that introduces the psalms before the start of the morning service. In בָּרוּךְ שֶׁאָמַר we praise the compassionate God "who spoke and the world came into being." Practice reading the selection from בָּרוּךְ שֶׁאָמַר aloud.

1. בָּרוּךְ שֶׁאָמַר וְהָיָה הָעוֹלָם.
2. בָּרוּךְ הוּא.
3. בָּרוּךְ עוֹשֶׂה בְרֵאשִׁית.
4. בָּרוּךְ אוֹמֵר וְעוֹשֶׂה.
5. בָּרוּךְ גּוֹזֵר וּמְקַיֵּם.
6. בָּרוּךְ מְרַחֵם עַל הָאָרֶץ.
7. בָּרוּךְ מְרַחֵם עַל הַבְּרִיּוֹת.
8. בָּרוּךְ מְשַׁלֵּם שָׂכָר טוֹב לִירֵאָיו.
9. בָּרוּךְ חַי לָעַד וְקַיָּם לָנֶצַח.
10. בָּרוּךְ פּוֹדֶה וּמַצִּיל.
11. בָּרוּךְ שְׁמוֹ.
12. בָּרוּךְ אַתָּה, יְיָ, מֶלֶךְ מְהֻלָּל בַּתִּשְׁבָּחוֹת.

Praised are You, Adonai, Ruler who is acclaimed with songs of praise.

Circle the words with the root אמר in the lines above.

How many words did you circle? ______

LESSON 5

וְזֹאת הַתּוֹרָה \ עֵץ חַיִּים הִיא \ עַל שְׁלֹשָׁה דְבָרִים

וְזֹאת הַתּוֹרָה

Before returning the Torah to the Ark, we raise it high so that the congregation can see its words. Read each Hebrew phrase in the right-hand column below. Write the word from the phrase that matches the English meaning in the left-hand column.

1. וְזֹאת הַתּוֹרָה	______ the Torah
2. אֲשֶׁר־שָׂם מֹשֶׁה	______ placed
3. לִפְנֵי בְּנֵי יִשְׂרָאֵל	______ people of Israel
4. עַל־פִּי יְיָ	______ Adonai
5. בְּיַד־מֹשֶׁה	______ Moses

Think About It!

Why do you think we raise the Torah for the entire congregation to see its words?

______

עֵץ חַיִּים הִיא

When we return the Torah to the Ark, the congregation stands and sings עֵץ חַיִּים הִיא ("It is a Tree of Life").

Use the words from the list below to fill in the blanks in the prayer.

דַּרְכֵי מְאֻשָּׁר שָׁלוֹם עֵץ נֹעַם דְּרָכֶיהָ חַיִּים

1. ______ ______ הִיא לַמַּחֲזִיקִים בָּהּ,

tree life

וְתֹמְכֶיהָ ______.

happy

2. ______ ______ ______, וְכָל־

its ways ways of pleasantness

נְתִיבוֹתֶיהָ ______.

peace

Endings

Complete the three words from the lines above that have the sound-alike ending ֶיהָ.

______כֶיהָ ______כֶיהָ ______תֶיהָ

Write the four words ending with a final ם.

______ ______ ______ ______

In Your Own Words

In what ways is the Torah a "tree of life"?

______

______

עַל שְׁלשָׁה דְבָרִים

Pirke Avot 1:2 teaches us, "The world stands on three things: on Torah, and on worship, and on acts of loving-kindness." These words have become part of the synagogue service in many congregations.

Write the Hebrew words in the correct order on the lines below, using the English as your guide.

עוֹמֵד   שְׁלשָׁה   הָעוֹלָם   דְבָרִים   עַל

________	________	________	________	________
stands	the world	things	three	on

The English phrases below are in the correct order. The Hebrew phrases are not. Number the Hebrew phrases to match their English meanings.

1. on Torah	וְעַל הָעֲבוֹדָה ___
2. and on worship	וְעַל גְּמִילוּת חֲסָדִים ___
3. and on acts of loving-kindness	עַל הַתּוֹרָה ___

Acts of Loving-Kindness: גְּמִילוּת חֲסָדִים

Choose an act of loving-kindness from below. Circle your choice. Then list three ways you can fulfill the mitzvah.

visiting the sick	בִּקּוּר חוֹלִים	hospitality	הַכְנָסַת אוֹרְחִים
honoring the elderly	הִדּוּר פְּנֵי זָקֵן	peace at home	שְׁלוֹם בַּיִת
good manners	דֶּרֶךְ אֶרֶץ	forgiveness	סְלִיחָה
preserving the environment	בַּל תַּשְׁחִית	all Israel is responsible for one another	כָּל יִשְׂרָאֵל עֲרֵבִים זֶה בָּזֶה

1. ________________________________
2. ________________________________
3. ________________________________

READING RULE

Double-Duty Dot

Sometimes the dot in the שׁ serves two purposes.
The dot identifies the letter שׁ and also serves as the vowel "o" for the letter that comes before the שׁ. This double-duty dot has the sound "o-sh" (חשֶׁךְ = שֶׁךְ + חֹ).

Rhythm Reading

Read each word below.

1. מֹשֶׁה   חֹשֶׁךְ   עֹשֶׁר
2. קָדֹשׁ   לִלְבֹּשׁ   לִפְרֹשׁ
3. נְחֹשֶׁת   שְׁלֹשָׁה   קְדֹשִׁים

Sometimes the dot in the שׂ serves two purposes.
The dot identifies the letter שׂ and also serves as the vowel "o" for the letter שׂ. This double-duty dot has the sound "so."

Rhythm Reading

Read each word below.

1. נָשׂא   שָׂשׂן   שׂטְנַי
2. חָשׂף   וַיֶּחֱשׂף   עשֶׂה

The Five Books of Moses

Genesis | Exodus | Leviticus | Numbers | **Deuteronomy**

The Book of Deuteronomy is largely devoted to Moses' address to the people before his death. He reviews their forty years of wandering in the desert and reminds them of their obligation to follow God's mitzvot. Read the verses below. Then answer the questions on the next page.

1. וַיֵּלֶךְ מֹשֶׁה וַיְדַבֵּר אֶת הַדְּבָרִים הָאֵלֶּה אֶל כָּל יִשְׂרָאֵל, ...וַיהוָה
אָמַר אֵלַי לֹא תַעֲבֹר אֶת הַיַּרְדֵּן הַזֶּה. (Deuteronomy 31:1, 2)

And Moses went and spoke these words to all of Israel, "...and Adonai has said to me, 'You shall not go across this Jordan (River).'"

2. וַיִּקְרָא מֹשֶׁה לִיהוֹשֻׁעַ וַיֹּאמֶר אֵלָיו לְעֵינֵי כָל יִשְׂרָאֵל חֲזַק וֶאֱמָץ
כִּי אַתָּה תָּבוֹא אֶת הָעָם הַזֶּה אֶל הָאָרֶץ... (Deuteronomy 31:7)

And Moses called to Joshua and said to him in the sight of all Israel, "Be strong and of good courage, for you shall go with this people to the land..."

3. וַיהוָה הוּא הַהֹלֵךְ לְפָנֶיךָ הוּא יִהְיֶה עִמָּךְ לֹא יַרְפְּךָ
וְלֹא יַעַזְבֶךָּ... (Deuteronomy 31:8)

"And Adonai will go before you. God will be with you. God will neither fail nor forsake you..."

4. וַיִּכְתֹּב מֹשֶׁה אֶת הַתּוֹרָה הַזֹּאת וַיִּתְּנָהּ אֶל הַכֹּהֲנִים...וְאֶל כָּל
זִקְנֵי יִשְׂרָאֵל. (Deuteronomy 31:9)

And Moses wrote down this teaching and gave it to the priests…and to all the elders of Israel.

5. וַיָּמָת שָׁם מֹשֶׁה עֶבֶד יְהוָֹה בְּאֶרֶץ מוֹאָב...וְלֹא קָם נָבִיא עוֹד
בְּיִשְׂרָאֵל כְּמֹשֶׁה אֲשֶׁר יְדָעוֹ יְהוָֹה פָּנִים אֶל פָּנִים. (Deuteronomy 34:5, 10)

And Moses, the servant of Adonai, died there, in the land of Moab…Never again did there arise in Israel a prophet like Moses whom Adonai knew face to face.

Torah Lesson

- Why do you think that Moses, having led the Jews through the desert for forty years, was not the one to take them into the Promised Land—Canaan?

- Why do you think that Moses announced "in the sight of all Israel" that Joshua was to lead them into the Promised Land?

- Name two things Moses did that made him a prophet like no other.

RECOGNIZING ROOTS

Below are the roots of the Hebrew words in the following exercise. Write each root next to its matching Hebrew word. Then write the English meaning.

עבד רחמ דרכ עשׂה ברכ קדש דבר עמד

		Root	English			Root	English
1.	עֲמִידָה	___ ___ ___	__________	5.	מַעֲשָׂיו	___ ___ ___	__________
2.	נְבָרֵךְ	___ ___ ___	__________	6.	עֲבָדִים	___ ___ ___	__________
3.	וְרַחוּם	___ ___ ___	__________	7.	יְדַבֵּרוּ	___ ___ ___	__________
4.	דְּרָכָיו	___ ___ ___	__________	8.	קָדְשׁוֹ	___ ___ ___	__________

Phrasing

Circle the word(s) in each phrase built on the root דרכ, עמד, or עבד.
Read the circled word aloud. Then read each phrase aloud.

1. עֲבָדִים הָיִינוּ לְפַרְעֹה בְּמִצְרָיִם
2. צַדִּיק יְהֹוָה בְּכָל דְּרָכָיו
3. דְּרָכֶיהָ דַרְכֵי נֹעַם
4. וְטַהֵר לִבֵּנוּ לְעָבְדְּךָ בֶּאֱמֶת
5. בְּאֵלִיָּהוּ הַנָּבִיא עַבְדֶּךָ
6. וּבְלֶכְתְּךָ בַדֶּרֶךְ
7. שֶׁבְּכָל דּוֹר וָדוֹר עוֹמְדִים עָלֵינוּ
8. וְעַל הָעֲבוֹדָה וְעַל גְּמִילוּת חֲסָדִים

Write the English meaning for each root below.

דרכ __________

עמד __________

עבד __________

אַשְׁרֵי

Psalm 145, a poem in praise of God, is part of the prayer service, where it is known as the אַשְׁרֵי. We recite the אַשְׁרֵי during the opening morning prayers, in the afternoon service, and, in some congregations, before concluding the Torah service.

Read the first and last lines from the אַשְׁרֵי.

אַשְׁרֵי יוֹשְׁבֵי בֵיתֶךָ; עוֹד יְהַלְלוּךָ סֶּלָה.

אַשְׁרֵי הָעָם שֶׁכָּכָה לּוֹ; אַשְׁרֵי הָעָם שֶׁיְיָ אֱלֹהָיו.

Happy are they that dwell in Your house; they will praise You forever.
Happy are the people that are so favored; happy are the people whose God is Adonai.

וַאֲנַחְנוּ נְבָרֵךְ יָהּ מֵעַתָּה וְעַד עוֹלָם. הַלְלוּיָהּ.

We will praise God now and forever. Halleluyah.

Insights

What do you think it means to "dwell" in God's house?

____

____

____

עָלֵינוּ

A Concluding Prayer

עָלֵינוּ, one of the concluding prayers of every service, is a pledge of loyalty to God. Fill in the missing words in the Hebrew phrases from עָלֵינוּ by using the words in the list below. (*Hint: The matching English words are underlined.*)
Practice reading the completed Hebrew phrases.

יִהְיֶה   מֶלֶךְ מַלְכֵי הַמְּלָכִים   עָלֵינוּ   וַאֲנַחְנוּ
הָאָרֶץ   לְשַׁבֵּחַ   וּמוֹדִים   בַּיּוֹם הַהוּא

1. ________ ________ לַאֲדוֹן הַכֹּל

It is our duty to praise the God of all

2. ________ כּוֹרְעִים וּמִשְׁתַּחֲוִים ________

And we bend the knee, bow, and give thanks

3. לִפְנֵי ________ ________ ________

Before the Ruler of rulers

4. וְהָיָה יְיָ לְמֶלֶךְ עַל כָּל ________

Adonai will rule all the land

5. ________ ________

On that day

6. ________ יְיָ אֶחָד וּשְׁמוֹ אֶחָד

Adonai will be One and God's name will be One

JUST FOR FUN

Play the Bingo game below to review the meaning of prayer words from lessons 1–6. Write the number of each English word over the matching Hebrew on the card. The first match has been made for you.

1. prophets
2. the nations
3. to praise
4. righteousness, justice
5. Zion
6. tree
7. the land
8. people of Israel
9. like You
10. Moses
11. worship
12. Ruler of rulers
13. Jerusalem
14. life
15. truth
16. acts of loving-kindness

צֶדֶק	חַיִּים	נְבִיאִים	9 כָּמוֹךָ
יְרוּשָׁלַיִם	אֱמֶת	צִיּוֹן	עֵץ
מֹשֶׁה	בְּנֵי יִשְׂרָאֵל	לְשַׁבֵּחַ	הָאָרֶץ
מֶלֶךְ מַלְכֵי הַמְּלָכִים	עֲבוֹדָה	גְּמִילוּת חֲסָדִים	הָעַמִּים

READING RULE

Ending with "ach"

- The vowel sound ַ is read first when חַ comes at the end of a word ("ach").

רוּחַ כֹּחַ לְשַׁבֵּחַ

Choose the correct word above to complete this phrase from עָלֵינוּ.

עָלֵינוּ ___________ לַאֲדוֹן הַכֹּל

It is our duty to praise the God of all

- When חַ comes at the end of a word, the accent is placed on the letter-vowel combination that comes before it.

לְשַׁ בֵּ חַ מַטְ בֵּ חַ לוּ חַ

WORD BUILDING

Read the word-parts. Then read the whole word. Remember the reading rule!

1. סוֹלֵ חַ סוֹלֵחַ
2. פּוֹתֵ חַ פּוֹתֵחַ
3. מָשִׁי חַ מָשִׁיחַ
4. שׁוֹלֵ חַ שׁוֹלֵחַ
5. לְהָנִי חַ לְהָנִיחַ
6. לְשַׁבֵּ חַ לְשַׁבֵּחַ
7. מְשַׂמֵּ חַ מְשַׂמֵּחַ
8. וּמַצְמִי חַ וּמַצְמִיחַ

Add the ending חַ ("ach") to complete each word below. First write the vowel ַ then the letter ח.

רוּ___ כֹּ___ מֹ___ אוֹרֵ___

הַמְנַבֵּ___ נְזַבֵּ___ נָשִׁי___ הַמִּזְבֵּ___

HOLIDAY CONNECTION

מָעוֹז צוּר is a popular חֲנֻכָּה song. Many of its words end with חַ. Practice reading those words on the following line.

לְשַׁבֵּחַ נְזַבֵּחַ מַטְבֵּחַ הַמְנַבֵּחַ הַמִּזְבֵּחַ

Now practice reading מָעוֹז צוּר. Can you sing it?

1. מָעוֹז צוּר יְשׁוּעָתִי
2. לְךָ נָאֶה לְשַׁבֵּחַ.
3. תִּכּוֹן בֵּית תְּפִלָּתִי
4. וְשָׁם תּוֹדָה נְזַבֵּחַ.
5. לְעֵת תָּכִין מַטְבֵּחַ
6. מִצָּר הַמְנַבֵּחַ.
7. אָז אֶגְמוֹר בְּשִׁיר מִזְמוֹר
8. חֲנֻכַּת הַמִּזְבֵּחַ.

Ḥanukkah Blessings

Practice reciting the three Ḥanukkah blessings.

1. בָּרוּךְ אַתָּה, יְיָ אֱלֹהֵינוּ, מֶלֶךְ הָעוֹלָם, אֲשֶׁר קִדְּשָׁנוּ בְּמִצְוֹתָיו
וְצִוָּנוּ לְהַדְלִיק נֵר שֶׁל חֲנֻכָּה.

2. בָּרוּךְ אַתָּה, יְיָ אֱלֹהֵינוּ, מֶלֶךְ הָעוֹלָם, שֶׁעָשָׂה נִסִּים לַאֲבוֹתֵינוּ
בַּיָּמִים הָהֵם בַּזְּמַן הַזֶּה.

On the first night only:

3. בָּרוּךְ אַתָּה, יְיָ אֱלֹהֵינוּ, מֶלֶךְ הָעוֹלָם, שֶׁהֶחֱיָנוּ וְקִיְּמָנוּ וְהִגִּיעָנוּ
לַזְּמַן הַזֶּה.

RECOGNIZING THE ROOT

The root of the word מֶלֶךְ ("ruler") is מלכ ("rule").

Read each of the following phrases. In each phrase, circle the word(s) built on the root מלכ.

1. לִקְרַאת שַׁבָּת הַמַּלְכָּה
2. אֲזַי מֶלֶךְ שְׁמוֹ נִקְרָא
3. יְיָ מֶלֶךְ יְיָ מָלָךְ יְיָ יִמְלֹךְ לְעוֹלָם וָעֶד
4. מֶלֶךְ מַלְכֵי הַמְּלָכִים
5. מַלְכוּתְךָ מַלְכוּת כָּל עוֹלָמִים
6. אָבִינוּ מַלְכֵּנוּ שְׁמַע קוֹלֵנוּ

Write the phrase from עָלֵינוּ. ______________________________

Comparisons

Read these words: מַלְאָךְ מֶלֶךְ

Which letter is different in the two words? ______

מַלְאָךְ means "angel" or "messenger." מַלְאֲכֵי means "angels of" or "messengers of."

מֶלֶךְ means "Ruler." מַלְכֵי means "Ruler of."

Read the following lines from שָׁלוֹם עֲלֵיכֶם.

שָׁלוֹם עֲלֵיכֶם, מַלְאֲכֵי הַשָּׁרֵת, מַלְאֲכֵי עֶלְיוֹן,
מִמֶּלֶךְ מַלְכֵי הַמְּלָכִים, הַקָּדוֹשׁ בָּרוּךְ הוּא.

Circle the Hebrew word meaning "angels" or "messengers." Draw a box around the phrase meaning "from the Ruler of rulers."

Now read the following verse from the Torah. Circle the Hebrew word for "angels" or "messengers."

וַיָּבֹאוּ שְׁנֵי הַמַּלְאָכִים סְדֹמָה בָּעֶרֶב... (Genesis 19:1)

And the two angels arrived in Sodom in the evening...

שָׁלוֹם עֲלֵיכֶם

A hymn is a song of praise to God. We sing the שָׁלוֹם עֲלֵיכֶם hymn on Friday night at home between lighting the Shabbat candles and reciting Kiddush. Some congregations sing שָׁלוֹם עֲלֵיכֶם during Friday evening services. In שָׁלוֹם עֲלֵיכֶם we sing of angels who come in peace, bless us with peace, and depart in peace.

1. שָׁלוֹם עֲלֵיכֶם, מַלְאֲכֵי הַשָּׁרֵת, מַלְאֲכֵי עֶלְיוֹן,
מִמֶּלֶךְ מַלְכֵי הַמְּלָכִים, הַקָּדוֹשׁ בָּרוּךְ הוּא.
2. בּוֹאֲכֶם לְשָׁלוֹם, מַלְאֲכֵי הַשָּׁלוֹם, מַלְאֲכֵי עֶלְיוֹן,
מִמֶּלֶךְ מַלְכֵי הַמְּלָכִים, הַקָּדוֹשׁ בָּרוּךְ הוּא.
3. בָּרְכוּנִי לְשָׁלוֹם, מַלְאֲכֵי הַשָּׁלוֹם, מַלְאֲכֵי עֶלְיוֹן,
מִמֶּלֶךְ מַלְכֵי הַמְּלָכִים, הַקָּדוֹשׁ בָּרוּךְ הוּא.
4. צֵאתְכֶם לְשָׁלוֹם, מַלְאֲכֵי הַשָּׁלוֹם, מַלְאֲכֵי עֶלְיוֹן,
מִמֶּלֶךְ מַלְכֵי הַמְּלָכִים, הַקָּדוֹשׁ בָּרוּךְ הוּא.

Peace upon you, O ministering angels, angels of the Supreme,
From the Ruler of rulers, the Holy Blessed One.

Come in peace, O angels of peace, angels of the Supreme,
From the Ruler of rulers, the Holy Blessed One.

Bless me with peace, O angels of peace, angels of the Supreme,
From the Ruler of rulers, the Holy Blessed One.

Depart in peace, O angels of peace, angels of the Supreme,
From the Ruler of rulers, the Holy Blessed One.

Be an Angel of Peace

Name one thing you can do to be an "angel" or "messenger" of peace.

____

____

LESSON 7

קַדִּישׁ

Mourner's Kaddish

The Mourner's Kaddish, קַדִּישׁ יָתוֹם, is recited in memory of those who have died. It does not mention death; rather, it is a prayer of praise to God. It ends with a wish for peace for all people. The קַדִּישׁ is written mostly in Aramaic, a language similar to Hebrew that was spoken by the Jews in the fifth century B.C.E. and for about a thousand years thereafter. The last two lines of the prayer are written in Hebrew.

Below are words from the קַדִּישׁ. Write the number of the matching English word below each Aramaic word. (*Hint: Look for prefixes and roots you know to make a match.*)

1. וּבְחַיֵּי ______ קַדִּישׁ ______ שְׁלָמָא ______ שְׁמֵהּ ______

2. וְיַמְלִיךְ ______ יִתְגַּדַּל ______ בְּרִיךְ ______ בְּעָלְמָא ______

1. peace
2. holy
3. in the world
4. (God's) name
5. will be great
6. blessed
7. and in the life of
8. and will rule

PRAYER FOR PEACE

The Aramaic part of the קַדִּישׁ concludes with a prayer for peace.

יְהֵא שְׁלָמָא רַבָּא מִן שְׁמַיָּא...

May there be great peace from heaven...

Circle the Aramaic word meaning "peace."

What is the root of the word? ___ ___ ___

The final lines of the קַדִּישׁ are a Hebrew prayer for peace.

עֹשֶׂה שָׁלוֹם בִּמְרוֹמָיו הוּא יַעֲשֶׂה שָׁלוֹם עָלֵינוּ וְעַל־כָּל־יִשְׂרָאֵל, וְאִמְרוּ אָמֵן.

May God who makes peace in the heavens, make peace for us and for all Israel. And say, Amen.

Circle the Hebrew word meaning "peace."

Think About It!

Why do you think we conclude the קַדִּישׁ with prayers for peace?

____

____

____

PATTERNS

Many words in the קַדִּישׁ begin with the prefix וְיִתְ.
Read each of the word-parts below. Add the prefix וְיִתְ to complete each word.
Then read the whole word.

1.	______פָּאַר	______רוֹמַם	______נַשֵּׂא
2.	______הַדַּר	______עַלֶּה	______הַלַּל

Now read aloud this complete sentence praising God.
Look for all the words beginning with וְיִתְ.

יִתְבָּרַךְ וְיִשְׁתַּבַּח וְיִתְפָּאַר וְיִתְרוֹמַם וְיִתְנַשֵּׂא וְיִתְהַדַּר וְיִתְעַלֶּה
וְיִתְהַלַּל שְׁמֵהּ דְּקֻדְשָׁא, בְּרִיךְ הוּא.

Blessed, praised, glorified, exalted, extolled, honored, magnified, and adored be the name of the Holy One, blessed is God.

Roots

Write the root for "bless." ___ ___ ___
Two words in the sentence praising God above are built on the root for "bless." Write them below.

________________ ________________

Write the root for "holy." ___ ___ ___

Which word in the sentence is built on the root for "holy"? ____________

MORE PATTERNS

Many words in the קַדִּישׁ conclude with the vowel and letter אָ, a common Aramaic ending.

Read the following Aramaic words aloud.

1.	רַבָּא	לְעֵלָּא	בַּעֲגָלָא	בִּרְכָתָא
2.	וְשִׁירָתָא	תֻּשְׁבְּחָתָא	וְנֶחֱמָתָא	בְּעָלְמָא
3.	שְׁלָמָא	שְׁמַיָּא	עָלְמַיָּא	דְּקֻדְשָׁא

Read the sentence below. Circle each word that ends with the vowel and letter אָ.

לְעֵלָּא מִן כָּל בִּרְכָתָא וְשִׁירָתָא, תֻּשְׁבְּחָתָא וְנֶחֱמָתָא דַּאֲמִירָן בְּעָלְמָא, וְאִמְרוּ אָמֵן.

God is beyond all the blessings, songs, adorations, and consolations that are spoken in the world, and say, Amen.

Roots

Which words in the sentence above are built on the root אמר ("speak" or "say")?

________________ ________________

Which word in the sentence above is built on the root ברכ ("bless")?

____

WORD WATCH

Many words, or different forms of a word, are repeated in the קַדִּישׁ.
Read the key word in each box. Then read each phrase aloud. Circle the key word, or a different form of the key word, as you find it in the phrase.

שְׁמֵהּ

1. יִתְגַּדַּל וְיִתְקַדַּשׁ שְׁמֵהּ רַבָּא
2. יְהֵא שְׁמֵהּ רַבָּא מְבָרַךְ
3. וְיִתְהַלַּל שְׁמֵהּ דְּקֻדְשָׁא

רַבָּא

4. יִתְגַּדַּל וְיִתְקַדַּשׁ שְׁמֵהּ רַבָּא
5. יְהֵא שְׁמֵהּ רַבָּא מְבָרַךְ
6. יְהֵא שְׁלָמָא רַבָּא מִן שְׁמַיָּא

אָמֵן

7. וּבִזְמַן קָרִיב וְאִמְרוּ אָמֵן
8. דַּאֲמִירָן בְּעָלְמָא וְאִמְרוּ אָמֵן
9. עָלֵינוּ וְעַל־כָּל־יִשְׂרָאֵל וְאִמְרוּ אָמֵן

שָׁלוֹם

10. יְהֵא שְׁלָמָא רַבָּא מִן שְׁמַיָּא
11. עֹשֶׂה שָׁלוֹם בִּמְרוֹמָיו
12. הוּא יַעֲשֶׂה שָׁלוֹם

חַי

13. בְּחַיֵּיכוֹן וּבְיוֹמֵיכוֹן וּבְחַיֵּי דְכָל־בֵּית יִשְׂרָאֵל

14. וְחַיִּים עָלֵינוּ וְעַל־כָּל־יִשְׂרָאֵל

יִשְׂרָאֵל

17. וּבְחַיֵּי דְכָל־בֵּית יִשְׂרָאֵל

18. וְעַל־כָּל־יִשְׂרָאֵל

מִן

15. לְעֵלָּא מִן כָּל־בִּרְכָתָא וְשִׁירָתָא

16. יְהֵא שְׁלָמָא רַבָּא מִן שְׁמַיָּא

בְּעָלְמָא

19. בְּעָלְמָא דִּי בְרָא כִרְעוּתֵהּ

20. לְעָלַם וּלְעָלְמֵי עָלְמַיָּא

21. תֻּשְׁבְּחָתָא וְנֶחֱמָתָא דַּאֲמִירָן בְּעָלְמָא

Forever and Ever

Practice reading the three-word phrase meaning "forever and ever."

לְעָלַם וּלְעָלְמֵי עָלְמַיָּא

Write the phrase to completee this sentence from the קַדִּישׁ.

יְהֵא שְׁמֵהּ רַבָּא מְבָרַךְ ____________ ____________

____________.

May God's great name be blessed forever and ever.

TAKING ROOT

The following roots all form the foundation for words in the קַדִּישׁ.
The English letters for each root are mixed up. Unscramble the letters and write the correct form of the English word under the matching Hebrew root. One has been filled in for you.

vrofere	loyh	slbes	cepea	kaem	ysa	eurl
עשה	מלכ	עלמ	אמר	ברכ	שלמ	קדש
________	________	forever	________	________	________	________

Each of the following words from the קַדִּישׁ is built on one of the roots above. Write the root under the word.

מַלְכוּתֵהּ	בְּעָלְמָא	מְבָרַךְ	וְיִתְקַדַּשׁ	.1
________	________	________	________	
שְׁלָמָא	בִּרְכָתָא	יִתְבָּרַךְ	קַדִּישׁ	.2
________	________	________	________	
דְּקֻדְשָׁא	וּלְעָלְמֵי	וְיַמְלִיךְ	וְאִמְרוּ	.3
________	________	________	________	
	יַעֲשֶׂה	עָלְמַיָּא	בְּרִיךְ	.4
	________	________	________	

קְדוּשָׁה

The קְדוּשָׁה, the third blessing in the עֲמִידָה, acknowledges God's holiness. The words קָדוֹשׁ, קָדוֹשׁ, קָדוֹשׁ ("holy, holy, holy") in the blessing are from the Book of Isaiah (6:3), where we read that winged angels praised God with these words. When we recite קָדוֹשׁ, קָדוֹשׁ, קָדוֹשׁ in the קְדוּשָׁה, we rise up on our toes three times and imagine we are like the angels elevating ourselves toward God.

Practice reading this selection from the קְדוּשָׁה.

1. נְקַדֵּשׁ אֶת־שִׁמְךָ בָּעוֹלָם, כְּשֵׁם שֶׁמַּקְדִּישִׁים אוֹתוֹ בִּשְׁמֵי מָרוֹם,
2. כַּכָּתוּב עַל יַד נְבִיאֶךָ: וְקָרָא זֶה אֶל־זֶה וְאָמַר:
3. קָדוֹשׁ, קָדוֹשׁ, קָדוֹשׁ יְיָ צְבָאוֹת, מְלֹא כָל־הָאָרֶץ כְּבוֹדוֹ.
4. בָּרוּךְ כְּבוֹד יְיָ מִמְּקוֹמוֹ.
5. יִמְלֹךְ יְיָ לְעוֹלָם, אֱלֹהַיִךְ צִיּוֹן, לְדֹר וָדֹר. הַלְלוּיָהּ!
6. לְדוֹר וָדוֹר נַגִּיד גָּדְלֶךָ, וּלְנֵצַח נְצָחִים קְדֻשָּׁתְךָ נַקְדִּישׁ.
7. וְשִׁבְחֲךָ, אֱלֹהֵינוּ, מִפִּינוּ לֹא יָמוּשׁ לְעוֹלָם וָעֶד.
8. בָּרוּךְ אַתָּה, יְיָ, הָאֵל הַקָּדוֹשׁ.

Root Review

Write:

- the root for קְדוּשָׁה ("holy"). ___ ___ ___
- the words in the קְדוּשָׁה built on that root.

_______________ _______________ _______________

_______________ _______________ _______________

LESSON 8

אֵין כֵּאלֹהֵינוּ

A Concluding Prayer

אֵין כֵּאלֹהֵינוּ, the joyful hymn that we sing near the end of the prayer service, is over 1,000 years old. The message of אֵין כֵּאלֹהֵינוּ, that there is no God like ours, is repeated throughout the song. The prayer describes our different relationships with God: God is our Sovereign, God is our Ruler, God is our Savior.

Match the Hebrew words in the list with the underlined English words to complete the Hebrew phrases. One answer has been filled in for you.

אֲדוֹנֵינוּ   מוֹשִׁיעֵנוּ   אֱלֹהֵינוּ   מַלְכֵּנוּ

You are our God — אַתָּה הוּא ________

You are our Sovereign — אַתָּה הוּא ________

You are our Ruler — אַתָּה הוּא ________

You are our Savior — אַתָּה הוּא מוֹשִׁיעֵנוּ

Word Skills

Write the suffix meaning "our." ______

Circle the prefix in each of the following words.

לֵאלֹהֵינוּ   כַּאדוֹנֵינוּ   כְּמַלְכֵּנוּ

MEMORY CHALLENGE

The verses of אֵין כֵּאלֹהֵינוּ are out of order.
Number the verses in the correct order of the prayer. The first one has been done for you. Then read the prayer in the correct order.

( ) בָּרוּךְ אֱלֹהֵינוּ, בָּרוּךְ אֲדוֹנֵינוּ,
בָּרוּךְ מַלְכֵּנוּ, בָּרוּךְ מוֹשִׁיעֵנוּ.

(1) אֵין כֵּאלֹהֵינוּ, אֵין כַּאדוֹנֵינוּ,
אֵין כְּמַלְכֵּנוּ, אֵין כְּמוֹשִׁיעֵנוּ.

( ) מִי כֵאלֹהֵינוּ, מִי כַאדוֹנֵינוּ,
מִי כְמַלְכֵּנוּ, מִי כְמוֹשִׁיעֵנוּ.

( ) אַתָּה הוּא אֱלֹהֵינוּ, אַתָּה הוּא אֲדוֹנֵינוּ,
אַתָּה הוּא מַלְכֵּנוּ, אַתָּה הוּא מוֹשִׁיעֵנוּ.

( ) נוֹדֶה לֵאלֹהֵינוּ, נוֹדֶה לַאדוֹנֵינוּ,
נוֹדֶה לְמַלְכֵּנוּ, נוֹדֶה לְמוֹשִׁיעֵנוּ.

Write the phrase meaning "There is none like our God." ____________________

RELIGIOUS POETRY

אֵין כֵּאלֹהֵינוּ is a *piyyut*, a religious poem. *Piyyutim* (plural) are distinguished by their rhyme or rhythm and acrostic lettering. In an acrostic, the initial letter of each line (or each half-line) spells out a word—often the author's name—or is part of a pattern of letters.

The acrostic in אֵין כֵּאלֹהֵינוּ spells the word אָמֵן.

In the אֵל אָדוֹן and אַשְׁרֵי prayers, you will find *alef-bet* acrostics in which each sentence begins with the next letter of the Hebrew alphabet.

לְכָה דוֹדִי is an acrostic spelling the author's name, שְׁלֹמֹה הַלֵּוִי.

Prayer Selections

Below are selections from the above mentioned *piyyutim*. Practice reading each one. Circle the *alef-bet* acrostic letters in אֵל אָדוֹן.

אֵל אָדוֹן

1. אֵל אָדוֹן עַל כָּל הַמַּעֲשִׂים   בָּרוּךְ וּמְבֹרָךְ בְּפִי כָּל נְשָׁמָה
2. גָּדְלוֹ וְטוּבוֹ מָלֵא עוֹלָם   דַּעַת וּתְבוּנָה סוֹבְבִים אֹתוֹ
3. הַמִּתְגָּאֶה עַל חַיּוֹת הַקֹּדֶשׁ   וְנֶהְדָּר בְּכָבוֹד עַל־הַמֶּרְכָּבָה
4. זְכוּת וּמִישׁוֹר לִפְנֵי כִסְאוֹ   חֶסֶד וְרַחֲמִים לִפְנֵי כְבוֹדוֹ

Circle the *alef-bet* acrostic letters in אַשְׁרֵי.

אַשְׁרֵי

1. אֲרוֹמִמְךָ אֱלוֹהַי הַמֶּלֶךְ, וַאֲבָרְכָה שִׁמְךָ לְעוֹלָם וָעֶד
2. בְּכָל־יוֹם אֲבָרְכֶךָּ, וַאֲהַלְלָה שִׁמְךָ לְעוֹלָם וָעֶד
3. גָּדוֹל יְיָ וּמְהֻלָּל מְאֹד, וְלִגְדֻלָּתוֹ אֵין חֵקֶר
4. דּוֹר לְדוֹר יְשַׁבַּח מַעֲשֶׂיךָ, וּגְבוּרֹתֶיךָ יַגִּידוּ
5. הֲדַר כְּבוֹד הוֹדֶךָ, וְדִבְרֵי נִפְלְאֹתֶיךָ אָשִׂיחָה

Circle the acrostic letters in לְכָה דוֹדִי to spell out the author's name, שְׁלֹמֹה הַלֵּוִי.

לְכָה דוֹדִי

1. שָׁמוֹר וְזָכוֹר בְּדִבּוּר אֶחָד...

2. לִקְרַאת שַׁבָּת לְכוּ וְנֵלְכָה...

3. מִקְדַּשׁ מֶלֶךְ עִיר מְלוּכָה...

4. הִתְנַעֲרִי מֵעָפָר קוּמִי...

5. הִתְעוֹרְרִי הִתְעוֹרְרִי...

6. לֹא תֵבֹשִׁי וְלֹא תִכָּלְמִי...

7. וְהָיוּ לִמְשִׁסָּה שֹׁאסָיִךְ...

8. יָמִין וּשְׂמֹאל תִּפְרֹצִי...

The Sabbath Bride

לְכָה דוֹדִי compares Shabbat to a bride. The *piyyut* begins with the following refrain which is repeated throughout.

לְכָה דוֹדִי לִקְרַאת כַּלָּה, פְּנֵי שַׁבָּת נְקַבְּלָה.

Let us go, my beloved, to meet the Bride, let us greet Shabbat.

When we sing the last verse of לְכָה דוֹדִי during the Friday evening service, we traditionally stand and face the back of the sanctuary to welcome the Shabbat bride. We bow to the left and to the right when we sing the last four words.

Practice reading the last verse of לְכָה דוֹדִי.

בּוֹאִי בְשָׁלוֹם עֲטֶרֶת בַּעְלָהּ, גַּם בְּשִׂמְחָה וּבְצָהֳלָה,
תּוֹךְ אֱמוּנֵי עַם סְגֻלָּה, בּוֹאִי כַלָּה, בּוֹאִי כַלָּה.

Come in peace, crown of your husband, in joy and in gladness,
In the midst of the faithful of the treasured people. Come, O Bride! Come, O Bride!

NAME THE PRAYER

Using the following list, write the name of each prayer selection on the blank line above it.

Then read each selection aloud.

בִּרְכוֹת הַתּוֹרָה   עָלֵינוּ   קַדִּישׁ   עַל שְׁלֹשָׁה דְבָרִים

1. ____________________

וַאֲנַחְנוּ כּוֹרְעִים וּמִשְׁתַּחֲוִים וּמוֹדִים

לִפְנֵי מֶלֶךְ מַלְכֵי הַמְּלָכִים, הַקָּדוֹשׁ בָּרוּךְ הוּא.

2. ____________________

יִתְבָּרַךְ וְיִשְׁתַּבַּח וְיִתְפָּאַר וְיִתְרוֹמַם וְיִתְנַשֵּׂא

וְיִתְהַדַּר וְיִתְעַלֶּה וְיִתְהַלַּל שְׁמֵהּ דְּקֻדְשָׁא, בְּרִיךְ הוּא.

3. ____________________

אֲשֶׁר בָּחַר־בָּנוּ מִכָּל־הָעַמִּים,

וְנָתַן־לָנוּ אֶת־תּוֹרָתוֹ.

בָּרוּךְ אַתָּה, יְיָ, נוֹתֵן הַתּוֹרָה.

4. ____________________

עַל הַתּוֹרָה וְעַל הָעֲבוֹדָה וְעַל גְּמִילוּת חֲסָדִים.

אֲדוֹן עוֹלָם

אֲדוֹן עוֹלָם is a concluding *piyyut* in the Shabbat morning service. It praises God and declares that God is eternal, without beginning or end. None can be compared to God.

Read the last word in each line to hear the rhythm and rhyme of the *piyyut*.
What is the vowel sound at the end of each line? _____
Practice reading the complete אֲדוֹן עוֹלָם.

1. אֲדוֹן עוֹלָם אֲשֶׁר מָלַךְ — בְּטֶרֶם כָּל־יְצִיר נִבְרָא.
2. לְעֵת נַעֲשָׂה בְחֶפְצוֹ כֹּל — אֲזַי מֶלֶךְ שְׁמוֹ נִקְרָא.
3. וְאַחֲרֵי כִּכְלוֹת הַכֹּל — לְבַדּוֹ יִמְלֹךְ נוֹרָא.
4. וְהוּא הָיָה וְהוּא הֹוֶה — וְהוּא יִהְיֶה בְּתִפְאָרָה.
5. וְהוּא אֶחָד וְאֵין שֵׁנִי — לְהַמְשִׁיל לוֹ לְהַחְבִּירָה.
6. בְּלִי רֵאשִׁית בְּלִי תַכְלִית — וְלוֹ הָעֹז וְהַמִּשְׂרָה.
7. וְהוּא אֵלִי וְחַי גּוֹאֲלִי — וְצוּר חֶבְלִי בְּעֵת צָרָה.
8. וְהוּא נִסִּי וּמָנוֹס לִי — מְנָת כּוֹסִי בְּיוֹם אֶקְרָא.
9. בְּיָדוֹ אַפְקִיד רוּחִי — בְּעֵת אִישַׁן וְאָעִירָה.
10. וְעִם רוּחִי גְּוִיָּתִי — יְיָ לִי וְלֹא אִירָא.

LESSON 9

הַשְׁכִּיבֵנוּ \ שְׁמַע \ מוֹדֶה אֲנִי

Evening and Morning Prayers

There are prayers we say when we go to sleep and prayers we say when we wake up. הַשְׁכִּיבֵנוּ, a prayer in the evening service, asks for God's protection throughout the night. In the morning, when we wake up, we say מוֹדֶה אֲנִי to thank God for restoring our souls to us and for giving us a new day. And the שְׁמַע, declaring our allegiance to God, is recited in the evening and in the morning at home and during services.

Evening

Use the words in the list below to complete this selection from הַשְׁכִּיבֵנוּ. The matching words are underlined in the English translation to assist you. (*Note: You may have to use a word more than once.*)
Then read the completed prayer aloud.

שָׁלוֹם   סֻכַּת   וְהַעֲמִידֵנוּ   שְׁלוֹמֶךָ   הַשְׁכִּיבֵנוּ

1. ___________ יְיָ אֱלֹהֵינוּ לְ___________, ___________
2. מַלְכֵּנוּ לְחַיִּים, וּפְרוֹשׂ עָלֵינוּ ___________ ___________...
3. וּשְׁמוֹר צֵאתֵנוּ וּבוֹאֵנוּ לְחַיִּים וּלְ___________ מֵעַתָּה וְעַד עוֹלָם.

Make us lie down, Adonai, in peace, and stand us up again,

our Ruler, to life, and spread upon us the shelter of Your peace...

And guard our going and our coming, for life and for peace now and forever.

Morning

Write the first six words of מוֹדֶה אֲנִי in the correct order.
(*Hint: Boys and men say* מוֹדֶה. *Girls and women say* מוֹדָה.)
Then read the complete prayer aloud.

לְפָנֶיךָ וְקַיָּם מוֹדֶה\מוֹדָה מֶלֶךְ אֲנִי חַי

__________ __________ __________ __________

__________ __________

שֶׁהֶחֱזַרְתָּ בִּי נִשְׁמָתִי בְּחֶמְלָה רַבָּה אֱמוּנָתֶךָ.

I give thanks to You, living and everlasting Ruler,
who has graciously returned my soul to me. Great is Your faithfulness!

Be a סוֹפֵר, Torah Scribe

When the שְׁמַע appears in the *sefer Torah*, it looks like this:

שמע ישראל יהוה אלהינו יהוה אחד

Practice reading the שְׁמַע. Notice how the Torah letters are different from the סִדּוּר. Circle God's name.

Be a Witness

Notice that the ע (שמע) and the ד (אחד) are larger than all the other letters. The two larger letters, ע and ד, spell the word עֵד ("witness").

What is the role of a witness? ______________________________

The English meaning of the שְׁמַע is: *Hear O Israel: Adonai is our God, Adonai is One.* How do you think one can be a witness that "Adonai is One"?

____

וְאָהַבְתָּ

The וְאָהַבְתָּ follows after the שְׁמַע in the Torah (Deuteronomy 6:4–9). Practice reading the וְאָהַבְתָּ.

1. וְאָהַבְתָּ אֵת יְיָ אֱלֹהֶיךָ
2. בְּכָל־לְבָבְךָ וּבְכָל־נַפְשְׁךָ וּבְכָל־מְאֹדֶךָ.
3. וְהָיוּ הַדְּבָרִים הָאֵלֶּה, אֲשֶׁר אָנֹכִי מְצַוְּךָ הַיּוֹם, עַל־לְבָבֶךָ.
4. וְשִׁנַּנְתָּם לְבָנֶיךָ, וְדִבַּרְתָּ בָּם בְּשִׁבְתְּךָ בְּבֵיתֶךָ,
5. וּבְלֶכְתְּךָ בַדֶּרֶךְ, וּבְשָׁכְבְּךָ וּבְקוּמֶךָ.
6. וּקְשַׁרְתָּם לְאוֹת עַל־יָדֶךָ, וְהָיוּ לְטֹטָפֹת בֵּין עֵינֶיךָ.
7. וּכְתַבְתָּם עַל־מְזֻזוֹת בֵּיתֶךָ וּבִשְׁעָרֶיךָ.

You shall love Adonai, your God,
with all your heart, and with all your soul, and with all your might.
Set these words, which I command you this day, upon your heart.
Teach them to your children, and speak of them when you are at home,
and when you go on your way, and when you lie down, and when you get up.
Bind them as a sign upon your hand and let them be symbols between your eyes.
Write them on the doorposts of your house and your gates.

Congregations usually recite another passage from the Torah, לְמַעַן תִּזְכְּרוּ, after the וְאָהַבְתָּ (Numbers 15:40–41). לְמַעַן תִּזְכְּרוּ reminds us to do the mitzvot. Practice reading the prayer.

1. לְמַעַן תִּזְכְּרוּ וַעֲשִׂיתֶם אֶת־כָּל־מִצְוֹתָי, וִהְיִיתֶם קְדֹשִׁים
2. לֵאלֹהֵיכֶם. אֲנִי יְיָ אֱלֹהֵיכֶם, אֲשֶׁר הוֹצֵאתִי אֶתְכֶם מֵאֶרֶץ
3. מִצְרַיִם לִהְיוֹת לָכֶם לֵאלֹהִים. אֲנִי יְיָ אֱלֹהֵיכֶם.

CROSSWORD PUZZLE

Complete the crossword puzzle using the English words below that match the numbered Hebrew roots.

rule compassion holy work way choose bless peace

4. שׁלמ	3. מלכ	2. עבד	1. דרכ
8. רחמ	7. ברכ	6. קדשׁ	5. בחר

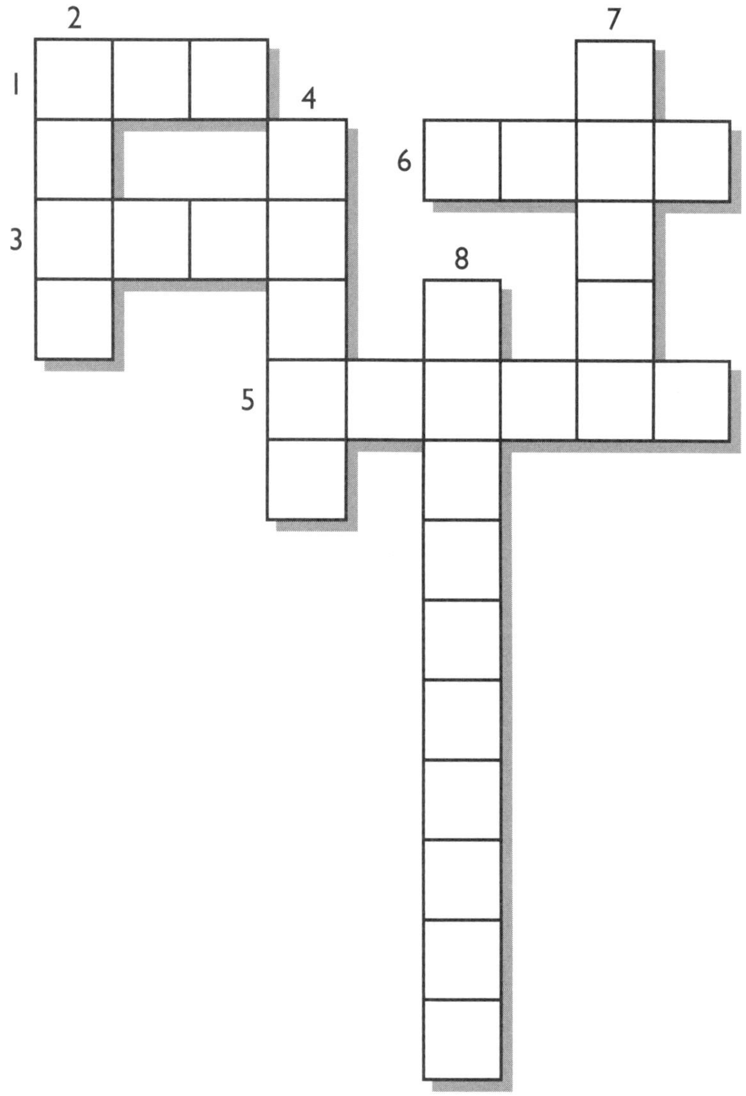

BUILDING BLOCKS

Write the number of each Hebrew line next to the matching English below it.
Read each Hebrew line aloud.

1. יְיָ מֶלֶךְ, יְיָ מָלָךְ, יְיָ יִמְלֹךְ לְעוֹלָם וָעֶד
2. גְּמִילוּת חֲסָדִים
3. לִפְנֵי בְּנֵי יִשְׂרָאֵל
4. מִירוּשָׁלָיִם
5. וּבְמֹשֶׁה עַבְדּוֹ
6. וַאֲנַחְנוּ כּוֹרְעִים וּמִשְׁתַּחֲוִים וּמוֹדִים
7. אֲשֶׁר נָתַן לָנוּ תּוֹרַת אֱמֶת
8. עֵץ חַיִּים הִיא לַמַּחֲזִיקִים בָּהּ

___ acts of loving-kindness

___ who gave us the Torah of truth

___ from Jerusalem

___ it is a tree of life to those who uphold it

___ and Moses, God's servant

___ before the people of Israel

___ Adonai is Ruler, Adonai ruled, Adonai will rule forever and ever

___ and we bend the knee, bow, and thank God

הַשְׁכִּיבֵנוּ

Practice reading the following lines from הַשְׁכִּיבֵנוּ.

1. הַשְׁכִּיבֵנוּ, יְיָ אֱלֹהֵינוּ, לְשָׁלוֹם, וְהַעֲמִידֵנוּ, מַלְכֵּנוּ, לְחַיִּים,
2. וּפְרוֹשׂ עָלֵינוּ סֻכַּת שְׁלוֹמֶךָ...
3. וּשְׁמוֹר צֵאתֵנוּ וּבוֹאֵנוּ לְחַיִּים
4. וּלְשָׁלוֹם, מֵעַתָּה וְעַד עוֹלָם, וּפְרוֹשׂ עָלֵינוּ סֻכַּת שְׁלוֹמֶךָ.
5. בָּרוּךְ אַתָּה, יְיָ, הַפּוֹרֵשׂ סֻכַּת שָׁלוֹם עָלֵינוּ, וְעַל־כָּל־עַמּוֹ
6. יִשְׂרָאֵל וְעַל יְרוּשָׁלָיִם.

A Shelter of Peace

The phrase, וּפְרוֹשׂ עָלֵינוּ סֻכַּת שְׁלוֹמֶךָ ("and spread upon us the shelter of Your peace"), or a variation, appears several times in the prayer.

Circle the phrases.

How many did you find? _______

Find a similar phrase in the last sentence and circle it.

How would you build a shelter of peace?

____

____

WRITING CHART

Script	Print	Name	Letter
		Alef	א
		Bet	בּ
		Vet	ב
		Gimmel	ג
		Dalet	ד
		Hay	ה
		Vav	ו
		Zayin	ז
		Ḥet	ח
		Tet	ט
		Yud	י
		Kaf	כּ
		Chaf	כ
		Final Chaf	ך
		Lamed	ל
		Mem	מ

Script	Print	Name	Letter
		Final Mem	ם
		Nun	נ
		Final Nun	ן
		Samech	ס
		Ayin	ע
		Pay	פּ
		Fay	פ
		Final Fay	ף
		Tsadee	צ
		Final Tsadee	ץ
		Koof	ק
		Resh	ר
		Shin	שׁ
		Sin	שׂ
		Tav	תּ
		Tav	ת